Where Does It Come From?

From Seed to Jam

by Penelope S. Nelson

Bullfrog Books

Ideas for Parents and Teachers

Bullfrog Books let children practice reading informational text at the earliest reading levels. Repetition, familiar words, and photo labels support early readers.

Before Reading

- Discuss the cover photo. What does it tell them?

- Look at the picture glossary together. Read and discuss the words.

Read the Book

- "Walk" through the book and look at the photos. Let the child ask questions. Point out the photo labels.

- Read the book to the child, or have him or her read independently.

After Reading

- Prompt the child to think more. Ask: Jam can be made from many fruits. Can you name different kinds of jam?

Bullfrog Books are published by Jump!
5357 Penn Avenue South
Minneapolis, MN 55419
www.jumplibrary.com

Library of Congress Cataloging-in-Publication Data

Names: Nelson, Penelope, 1994– author.
Title: From seed to jam / Penelope S. Nelson.
Description: Minneapolis: Jump!, Inc., [2021]
Series: Where does it come from?
Audience: Ages 5–8. | Audience: Grades K–1.
Identifiers: LCCN 2019053329 (print)
LCCN 2019053330 (ebook)
ISBN 9781645275381 (library binding)
ISBN 9781645275398 (paperback)
ISBN 9781645275404 (ebook)
Subjects: LCSH: Strawberries—Preservation—Juvenile literature. | Jam—Juvenile literature.
Canning and preserving—Juvenile literature.
Classification: LCC TX612.J3 N45 2021 (print)
LCC TX612.J3 (ebook) | DDC 641.4/2—dc23
LC record available at https://lccn.loc.gov/2019053329
LC ebook record available at https://lccn.loc.gov/2019053330

Editor: Jenna Gleisner
Designer: Anna Peterson

Photo Credits: Volosina/Shutterstock, cover; beboy/Shutterstock, 1; Moon Light PhotoStudio/Shutterstock, 3; a454/Shutterstock, 4; Bukhta Yurii/Shutterstock, 5; Nelli Syrotynska/Shutterstock, 6, 22tl; g215/Shutterstock, 6–7, 22tr; Androniques/Dreamstime, 8–9, 22mr, 23br; Inti St Clair/Getty, 10, 22br, 23bl; kameleon777/iStock, 11 (top); Alekseykolotvin/Shutterstock, 11 (bottom); Westend61/Getty, 12–13 (pot); NIKCOA/Shutterstock, 12–13 (sugar); New Africa/Shutterstock, 12–13 (lemons); Jeremy Reddington/Shutterstock, 12–13 (background); margouillat photo/Shutterstock, 14; Nitr/Shutterstock, 15; ppart/Shutterstock, 16–17 (pot), 22bl, 23tl; traction/Shutterstock, 16–17 (strawberries), 22bl, 23tl, 23tr; Sheila Fitzgerald/Dreamstime, 18–19; Maja Marjanovic/Shutterstock, 19, 22ml; Hill Street Studios/Getty, 20–21 (stand); CL Shebley/Shutterstock, 20–21 (jams); lozas/Shutterstock, 24.

Printed in the United States of America at Corporate Graphics in North Mankato, Minnesota.

Table of Contents

Sweet and Fruity

Jen loves jam.

Where does it come from?

strawberry

Fruit!

Like what?

Strawberries!

They start as tiny seeds.

They grow into plants.

seeds

plants

Berries grow.

They ripen.

We pick them.

We rinse the berries.

pot

We cut them.

We put them in a pot.

lemon
juice

sugar

12

We add sugar.

Lemon juice goes in next.

We stir!

We can use other berries!
Like what?
Blackberries.

blackberry

Raspberries, too.

raspberry ·····▶

We heat the mixture.

It boils.

It turns into jam!

jar

We pour it into jars.
It cools.
Tom puts it on toast.
Yum!

Meg sells some.

Do you like jam?

From Fruit to Table

How does strawberry jam get to our tables?

1. Strawberry seeds are planted.

2. They grow into plants. Berries grow.

3. Ripe berries are picked.

4. The berries are rinsed, cut, and mixed with other ingredients.

5. The mixture is boiled and turns into jam.

6. It is put in jars and ready to eat after it has cooled.

Picture Glossary

boils
Heats to the point where it bubbles.

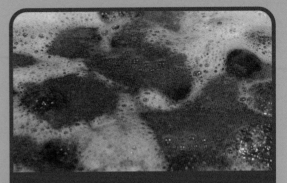

mixture
A combination of different things mixed together.

rinse
To get rid of dirt by washing something with clean water.

ripen
To fully develop and be ready to be picked.

Index

To Learn More

FACT SURFER

Finding more information is as easy as 1, 2, 3.

❶ Go to www.factsurfer.com

❷ Enter "fromseedtojam" into the search box.

❸ Choose your book to see a list of websites.